Madagascar

Mary N. Oluonye

🌱 Carolrhoda Books, Inc. / Minneapolis

Photo Acknowledgments

Photos, maps, and artworks are used courtesy of: John Erste, pp. 1, 2–3, 14, 16–17, 20–21, 22–23, 28–29, 32–33, 37, 38–39; Laura Westlund, pp. 4, 33; © Victor Englebert, pp. 4, 6, 7, 8, 9, 16, 17, 20, 22, 25 (top), 26, 27, 28 (both), 29, 31, 34, 35, 40 (both), 41, 42, 43, 44; © Eugene G. Schulz, pp. 10, 11 (both), 12 (both), 13, 14, 18, 24, 25 (bottom), 36 (both), 45; Alton Halverson, p. 19 (inset); © The American Lutheran Church, used by permission of Augsburg Fortress, pp. 19, 23; © H. Bradt/C.O.P., p. 30. Cover photo of roadside vendors © Victor Englebert.

Carolrhoda Books, Inc.
A Division of Lerner Publishing Group
241 First Avenue North
Minneapolis, Minnesota 55401 U.S.A.

Website address: www.lernerbooks.com

Words in **bold type** are explained in a glossary that begins on page 44.

Library of Congress Cataloging-in-Publication Data

Oluonye, Mary N.
      Madagascar / by Mary N. Oluonye
          p. cm.—(Globe-trotter's club)
      Includes index.
      Summary: Examines the history, society, economy, and culture of Madagascar.
        ISBN 1–57505–120–6 (lib.bdg. : alk. paper)
        1. Madagascar—Juvenile literature. I. Title II. Series: Globe-trotters club (series)
DT469.M26 048 2000
969.1—dc21   98–54225

Manufactured in the United States of America
1 2 3 4 5 6 – JR – 05 04 03 02 01 00

Contents

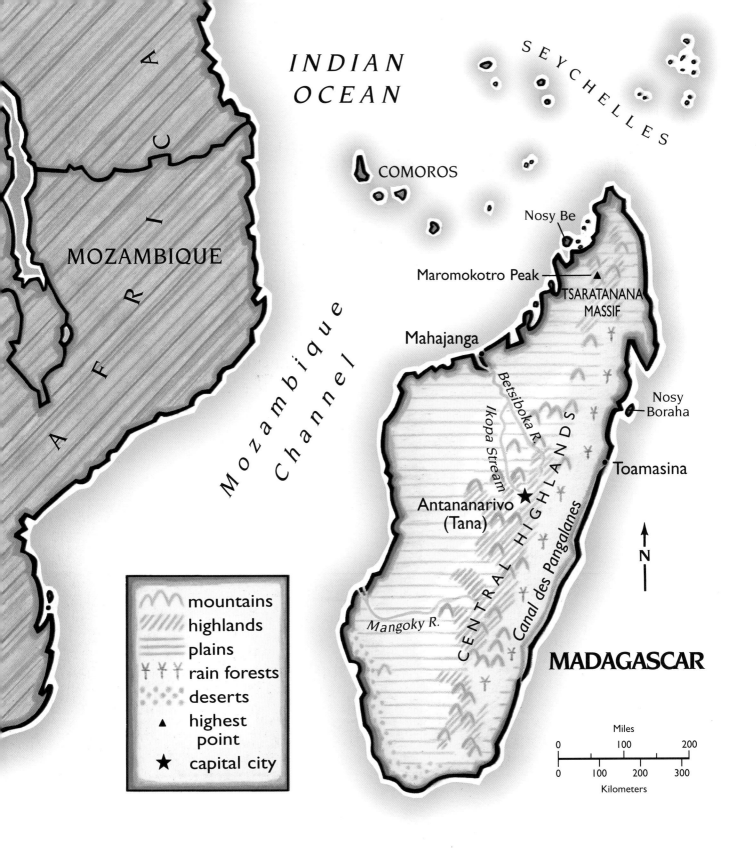

Tongasoa eto
Madagasikara!*

That's "Welcome to Madagascar!" in Malagasy, one of the two official languages of Madagascar.

Just a hop, skip, and a jump from the coast of south-eastern Africa, you'll find the island country of Madagascar. With an area of more than 226,000 square miles, Madagascar is the fourth largest island in the world. Madagascar could be a puzzle piece that fits easily into the coast of Mozambique—a country in southeast Africa. In fact millions of years ago, the island broke away from Africa and slowly drifted eastward into the Indian Ocean.

MASCARENE ISLANDS

The Indian Ocean washes most of Madagascar's coast. To the west, the Mozambique Channel separates Madagascar from Africa. Madagascar's neighbors are the Mascarene Islands to the east, and the island countries of Comoros to the northwest and Seychelles to the northeast.

The green landscape of southern Madagascar meets the turquoise water of the Indian Ocean.

The Evatra River, which runs across southeastern Madagascar, empties into the Indian Ocean near the city of Tôlañaro.

Island **Scapes**

If you were to hike across Madagascar from west to east, the beginning and end of your trip would be easy. You'd start out crossing flat **plains,** dotted with sandy beaches and swamps, which line the west coast.

Hope you're up for a climb! To get to the middle of the island, you'll have to hike the Central Highlands. This spine of mountains runs the length of Madagascar. The highest point on the island is Maromokotro Peak, a mountain located in the northern Tsaratanana Massif (range). It towers to a lofty 9,436 feet.

It's all downhill to the east coast, where the land flattens out again. Lots of rainfall in this region has created the island's lush **rain forests.** Unlike the western coast, which is carved with inlets and bays, the eastern coast shoreline is so straight, it looks as if someone drew it with a ruler. The **Canal** des Pangalanes, a natural waterway formed by Indian Ocean currents, spans 500 miles of the eastern coast.

Fast Facts about Madagascar

Official Name: Republic of Madagascar

Area: 226,658 square miles

Major Landforms: Central Highlands, Tsaratanana Massif, Nosy Boraha Island

Highest Point: Maromokotro Peak (9,436 feet)

Lowest Point: Sea level

Major Rivers: Mangoky River, Betsiboka River, Ikopa Stream

Major Lakes: Lake Alaotra, Lake Itasy

Capital City: Antananarivo

Other Major Cities: Toamasina, Mahajanga

Official Languages: Malagasy, French

Money Unit: Malagasy franc

Madagascar's broad plains stretch for miles and miles until they reach mountains.

Weather or Not

Madagascar has two seasons—a hot, rainy season and a cooler, dry season. The hot, rainy season is also known as the Malagasy summer. It lasts from November to April. During this time, temperatures range from 61 to 84 degrees. Wet **monsoons** from the Indian Ocean blow across the island, carrying thick storm clouds that dump lots of rain on Madagascar's eastern coast. **Cyclones,** intense storms similar to tornadoes, form out in the ocean and whip heavy rains and winds across the island. They are most likely to strike between December and March.

A rain shower soaks a village during Madagascar's wet summer season.

During the Malagasy summer, trade winds carry rain across Madagascar.

The hot winter sun beats down on a group of travelers.

The Malagasy winter lasts from May through October, and many people say that this is the best time to visit Madagascar. During these months, the bright sun shines almost every day. Daytime temperatures average 78 degrees, but they cool off at night. July is Madagascar's coolest month, with average temperatures of 65 degrees.

Killer Winds

On February 2, 1994, Cyclone Geralda blew across Madagascar for two days. About 100 people were killed, and 500,000 people lost their homes. Floods washed away many rice fields, roads, and railroads, especially on the eastern half of the island.

A World **Apart**

Travelers to Madagascar see animals that can be found nowhere else in the world. How did these creatures get there? When Madagascar broke away from Africa, the living things on the island remained cut off from the rest of the world for millions of years. During that time, many of the plants and animals that became **extinct** in other parts of the world continued to live, grow, and change in Madagascar.

The lemur is one of the island's most well-known animals. You may have seen lemurs at the zoo—they look like a mix between a monkey and a raccoon. Lemurs sleep during the day and have big, round eyes to help them see through the darkest of nights. In Madagascar you'll find 40 different kinds of lemurs.

The word *lemur* means "nighttime spirit" in Latin.

Madagascar is also home to 700 types of butterflies, half the world's population of chameleons (a kind of lizard), and an ancient fish called the coelacanth. These fish lived during the days of the dinosaurs. They swim through the cold, underwater caves of the Mozambique Channel. Before discovering the fish in 1938, scientists thought that coelacanths had been extinct for millions of years.

The Elephant Bird

Have you ever heard of a bird that's 10 feet tall and weighs 1,000 pounds? The aepyornis, a creature that lived on the island of Madagascar long ago, fits that description perfectly. Humans hunted the birds until the aepyornis became extinct about 300 years ago. One complete bird skeleton and several egg fossils are on display at the Tsimbazaza Zoological and Botanical Gardens in the city of Antananarivo. The aepyornis laid eggs so big they could hold two gallons of water!

A chameleon clings to a branch in Madagascar's rain forest. Chameleons change color to blend into their surroundings.

Handy **Plants**

Feeling ill? The periwinkle plant (above) **may hold the perfect cure. But if you're just thirsty, look for the traveler's tree** (left). **The tree's trunk holds water like a canteen. The water tastes awful, but it will quench your thirst.**

 Plants found on Madagascar have been used to treat a lot of illnesses. For example, the periwinkle plant—a creeping evergreen plant with oval, shiny dark green leaves and blue or white flowers—contains chemicals that have been used to treat diabetes, bleeding problems, coughing, sore throats, eye infections, high blood pressure, and childhood leukemia. Periwinkle plants were once found only on the island of Madagascar. But these days, people grow the useful plant wherever it is warm. Another Malagasy plant, the katrafay, can be soaked in bath water and used to ease tired muscles. Bark from a kily tree soothes measles and rheumatism, a disease that causes painful swelling in the joints and muscles.

Many other Malagasy plants bear great-tasting foods. Banana, mango, and coffee trees all thrive in Madagascar. Vanilla, used to flavor ice cream and many other sweets, comes from the fruit of an orchid—a rain-forest flower. Farmers also grow orchards of clove trees—the dried, ground blossoms of which spice up pumpkin pies.

Plants That Bite

Not all plants in Madagascar are tasty or useful. In the desertlike southern part of the island, cactuses and thorny trees take over. A few of these plants have sharp thorns and poisons that protect them from birds and other natural enemies. Some of the poisons can burn a person's skin and may even cause blindness. Be sure to steer clear of these prickly plants!

Modern-day Malagasy people paddle a canoe similar to the boats their ancestors used to get to the island.

First **People**

As many as 1,500 years ago, the first people to set foot on the island of Madagascar arrived in large canoes. These folks were the **ancestors** of the Malagasy people. Although no books or journals can tell us about these travelers, scientists have used clues to figure out that the Malagasy came from islands located 4,000 miles east of Madagascar. Can you imagine canoeing that far across the ocean? People from the Southeast Asian countries of Indonesia and Malaysia share similar physical traits—such as hair and eye color—and traditions with the Malagasy.

When the original settlers arrived, some of them moved to the Central Highlands, where the climate and land were suitable for farming. They came to be called the Merina, which means "people of the highlands." In time Africans settled in Madagascar, too. They lived along the coasts and traded with people from Africa and the Comoros Islands to the north-west. These folks were known as the Betsimisaraka, which means "a large group of people who stick together."

India

Africa

Malaysia

Indonesia

Madagascar

What Route Did They Take?

Some experts believe that Indonesians sailed directly to Madagascar. Others think that they stopped in India and East Africa first. There they may have rested and picked up supplies and more passengers before going on to Madagascar.

We Are **Malagasy**

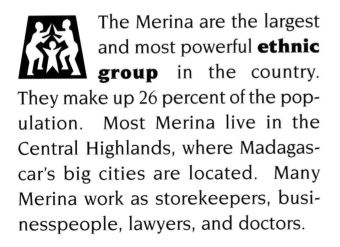

This monument is dedicated to Madagascar's 18 ethnic groups.

The Merina are the largest and most powerful **ethnic group** in the country. They make up 26 percent of the population. Most Merina live in the Central Highlands, where Madagascar's big cities are located. Many Merina work as storekeepers, businesspeople, lawyers, and doctors.

The Betsimisaraka are the second largest group, making up 15 percent of the population. They live on the eastern coast of Madagascar, and most fish or trade for a living. About 12 percent of the population belong to the Betsileo group. Their name means "big group that can't be conquered." Like the Merina people, the Betsileo live in the Central Highlands. They are the best farmers in the country, growing coffee beans, rice, and sweet potatoes. Other Malagasy ethnic groups include the Tsimihety, the Sakalava, the Antandroy, and the Bara.

But the Malagasy people aren't the only ones who call Madagascar home. Newcomers from Comoros, France, India, Pakistan, and China live there, too.

A Young Country

More than half of the Malagasy population is 20 years old or younger. In fact, 1999 figures show that 44 percent of the people of Madagascar are 15 years old or younger! Why so many kids? The government in Madagascar has encouraged families to have lots of children, because it believes that the country needs more people in order to grow and develop.

A Betsileo brother and sister

Many Faiths

The steeple of this Catholic church rises high into the air. Even those who follow the traditional religion sometimes go to church.

About 40 percent of the Malagasy are Christians. Europeans introduced Christianity to the islanders in the 1800s. These days almost half of Malagasy Christians are Roman Catholic, and the rest are Protestants. About 5 percent of Madagascar's population are Muslims who follow the teachings of Islam. Most Mala-gasy Muslims are descendants of settlers from Comoros and India. They tend to live in cities and towns along the northern coast.

Just over half of the Malagasy people follow the traditional religion of Madagascar. They believe that one supreme god, known as Zanahary (Creator) or Andriamanitra (Sweet Lord) rules everything. Lesser spirits dwell in animals, tombs, houses, trees, and water. A big part of Malagasy traditional religion is ancestor worship. Ancestors, known as *razana*, are believed to watch over living people and to teach them how best to live their lives. The razana can also ask Zanahary to bless or punish people for their actions. The Malagasy go out of their way to honor and respect the razana so they won't be punished.

On Fridays and holidays, Muslims come to pray at mosques—Islamic places of worship.

Cattle horns, ritual carvings, and food offerings mark the tombs of islanders who followed Madagascar's traditional religion.

Miteny Gasy
ve Ianao?

That means, "Do you speak Malagasy?" in the Malagasy language. If your answer is *eny* (yes), you'll have no problem getting around in Madagascar.

Even though Madagascar is home to 18 different ethnic groups, they all speak the same language. Malagasy shares words in common with Indonesian languages, but it also borrows words from Arabic, English, French, and from several other African languages. The Malagasy alphabet is similar to the English alphabet, except it doesn't have the letters *c*, *q*, *u*, *w*, or *x*.

People can choose to read newspapers in French or in Malagasy.

q, U, W, X

Talk to a Malagasy

Here are a few words and phrases that will help you get by in Madagascar. Practice your Malagasy with a friend.

English	Malagasy	
Hello	Manoa ahoana	MAH-noh OHN
How are you?	Fahasalamana?	fah-sah-lah-MAHN-ah
Please	Aza fady tompoko	AH-zah FAH-dee TOOM-poo-kuh
Thank you	Misaotra	mees-OW-tr
Good-bye	Veloma	veh-LOOM
Yes	Eny	AY-nee
No	Tsia	TSEE-yah

In Malagasy cities, you'll be able to talk to a few people if you speak French. Malagasy and French are the country's two official languages. French became a main language on the island in 1896, when France took over Madagascar. Even though Madagascar became an independent country on June 26, 1960, French is still a useful language to know how to write and speak. Malagasy is the language used in schools, but many students continue to study French. The Malagasy use French in business, in government, and in the universities. Malagasy citizens who speak fluent French often end up getting better and higher-paying jobs.

Wear **This**

Three men sport lambas—the symbol of Malagasy culture from birth to death.

Clothing in Madagascar hasn't changed much since the first settlers arrived. People wear **lambas**—long pieces of fabric that drape across the body and tie at the shoulder.

In the past, men wore lambas tied around their waists over a **loincloth.** Women wore their lambas over a long piece of fabric that they wrapped around themselves. Modern Malagasy women and girls just tie lambas over dresses or tops and skirts. (They never wear pants.) Men and boys put on shirts and shorts or pants under their lambas. In the big cities of Madagascar, many people choose to skip the lamba altogether.

Malagasy women weave lambas from silk, cotton, wool, or even grass on a special device called a Merina **loom.** Weavers create lambas in all sorts of colors, sizes, and designs—including landscapes, fruits, flowers, and geometric patterns. Folks from the Merina ethnic group prefer white lambas, while other groups might wear bright red, bright blue, or multicolored lambas.

A woman weaves a new lamba of goats' wool.

23

Many rural homes don't have running water, so women and children must draw water at the town well.

Country **Living**

The majority of the Malagasy people live in rural areas—in small towns and villages where they can be near family and friends. Malagasy communities, called *fakonolona*, are close knit, and family is very important. Kids might live with brothers and sisters, parents, grandparents, great-grandparents, uncles, aunts, and cousins. Family members who don't share the same house usually live close by. Everyone is expected to cooperate and to help one another. From an early age, Malagasy kids learn to respect their grandparents and other elders in the fakonolana.

Malagasy women usually marry and have kids when they are teenagers. When the kids get old enough, they help their mothers tend the garden. Families grow enough food to feed themselves. They may sell or trade extra food for pots, pans, or other household items. At one time, many of the men in Madagascar herded zebus (cows with humped backs and big horns) for a living. People still measure wealth by the number of zebus they own. These days island men work in big rice fields or hold office jobs.

All in the Family

Here are the Malagasy words for family members. Practice using these terms on your own family. See if they can understand you!

grandfather	*dadabe*	(dah-dah-BAY)
grandmother	*nenibe*	(neh-nee-BAY)
father	*dada*	(DAH-dah)
mother	*neny*	(NEE-nee)
uncle	*dadatoa*	(dah-dah-TOO-ah)
aunt	*nenitoa*	(nee-nee-TOO-ah)
son	*zanaka lahy*	(ZAH-nah-kah LYE)
daughter	*zanaka vavy*	(ZAH-nah-kah VAH-vee)
brother	*rahalahy*	(rah-hah-LAH-hee)
sister	*rahavavy*	(rah-hah-VAH-vee)

At the end of the day, rural people unhitch their zebus. It's time for both people and animals to relax.

25

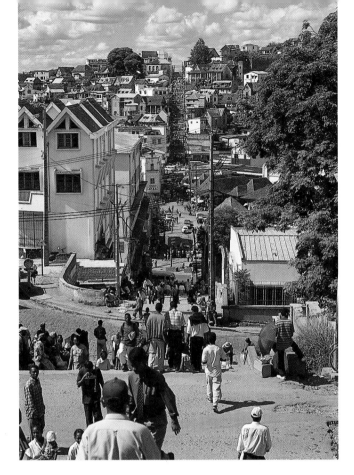

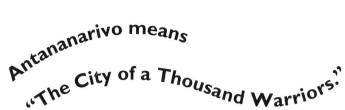

Antananarivo means "The City of a Thousand Warriors."

The streets of Antananarivo sure are steep!

City **Slickers**

The biggest city in Madagascar is Antananarivo, the country's capital. Malagasy people call the city Tana for short. As a city of nearly one million people, Antananarivo is crowded and busy. Brightly colored brick or wood houses, squeezed into tight rows, blanket the city's hillsides. Many homes are two or three stories tall with steep, pitched roofs. Some people can afford to own French-style brick homes with red tile roofs and balconies. Narrow stone alleys, streets, and stairs wind between the houses and up and down the hills.

It was named in 1610 when a Merina king sent 1,000 men to defend the area.

Tana's buildings and streets crowd around Lake Anosy, found in the city's center.

One particular set of stairs is so steep that it's called Tsia Fakantitra, which means "Old folks can't make it."

Most of the people living in Antananarivo are poor. They work hard in retail shops or as street ven-dors, taxi drivers, and bus drivers. Some folks labor on farms or in small factories in and around the city. Others don't have jobs and must spend the days begging for money around the city.

Getting **There**

Don't expect to zip from place to place by car in Madagascar. Although some Malagasy people do own cars, poor roads make travel bumpy and slow. Heavy rain often washes out the dirt

A group of kids (above) use Madagascar's most popular form of transportation— their feet. Other people have decided to ride a taxi-brousse (left). Pile in!

roads that crisscross the island. Streets rutted with potholes make for a bouncy ride. Needless to say, most people choose to walk. Others may ride in a cart or wagon pulled by zebus.

In cities where it's not too hilly, you can catch a ride in a *pousse pousse*. A pousse pousse (meaning "push, push" in French) is a two-wheeled, covered cart that's pulled by a driver. If you don't mind waiting, you can travel in a *taxi-brousse*—a vehicle that can hold a lot of people. Although taxi-brousses are supposed to run on a schedule, drivers usually wait until they have a full load of passengers before leaving. Be prepared to feel like a sardine packed in a can—these trucks or minibuses are crowded!

Riders can take it easy, but pousse pousse drivers are running all day! It's easy to see why a pousse pousse can't be found in a hilly city like Antananarivo.

Celebrating with
Ancestors

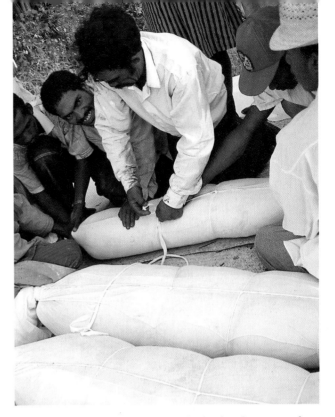

This family has wrapped their deceased relatives in new, white lambas. Some Malagasy mix Christian and traditional beliefs. During famadihana, these people might take their ancestors to church for a special service.

Merina people show respect for the dead by holding a ceremony called *famadihana*, which means "the turning of the bones." According to the famadihana tradition, family members open the loved one's tomb, remove the old lamba, wash the body, and wrap it in a new silk lamba.

Although the ceremony can be difficult and sad, it is also a time to celebrate—kind of like a family reunion. Families hire a band and **sacrifice** cattle for the two-day event. Relatives and friends gather to eat, sing, and dance. Partygoers make it a point to talk to the body, and some might even dance with the ancestor. At the end of the ceremony, the body is buried again in the same place. Because famadihana is an expensive ceremony, families host such an event only as often as they can afford to—usually every three, five, or seven years.

A Malagasy Funeral

In the Malagasy culture, a funeral is a big event. When a person dies, family members take his or her body to the family's home village and bury it with their ancestors. To prepare the body for burial, family members wash it and cover it with a white cloth. For a few days, the body remains at the family home so that family members and friends may pay their respects. Before burial the body is wrapped in a silk lamba. The body is laid in a tomb or underground chamber that is often sturdier than most Malagasy homes.

These castlelike structures are actually decorated tombs.

Party at the *Top*

What's your favorite holiday? Everyone in Madagascar loves to celebrate the new year. The first new moon of the year marks the Malagasy new year, called Alahamady. It's the most popular holiday in Madagascar. In the city of Tana, Alahamady is a two-day event. On New Year's Eve, people put on their best holiday clothes and colorful lambas. They walk to the highest point in the town. Up high they give each other gifts, mingle, listen to music, sing, and call upon the spirits of their ancestors as the new year arrives. The next morning, many Malagasy gather at church to sing songs and attend a service.

Malagasy Independence Day is June 26. It commemorates Madagascar's independence from France on that day in 1960. Schoolchildren sing the national anthem and parade through the streets with banners. Friends and family get together later in the evening to party and feast.

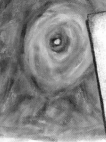

Dear Mom and Dad,

Fahasalamana? That's "How are you" in Malagasy. I'm having the best time visiting Grandma and Grandpa in Madagascar. Yesterday we climbed the royal hill of Ambohimanga in Tana to celebrate the Malagasy new year. Here they call it Alahamady. Grandma even gave me a lamba to wear over my clothes, but I had to leave my tennis shoes at home. She said it's impolite to wear shoes to the party. There were so many people there, but we all crowded into what used to be the queen's palace. We listened to loud music and danced. It was lots of fun.

See you soon!

Sun Mainitian
Waum Kaillian
Thaturhin, Sumbu
F30N, Lauratten

In rural Madagascar, where rice cultivation is a major part of daily life, celebrations such as the Festival of Rice are more meaningful than national holidays. Held in February, the festival gives thanks for a successful harvest.

Sidetrack

Christians in Madagascar celebrate Christmas, too. Instead of Santa Claus, there is Father Christmas—called Bonhomme Noël in French and Dadabenoely in Malagasy.

Get to **Class**

Until almost 200 years ago, Malagasy kids didn't go to school. Instead they learned traditions and customs by watching their parents, grandparents, and community elders.

These days all Malagasy children between the ages of 6 and 14 must go to school. Kids have to wake up early to make it to class by 7:00 A.M. They study French, science, math, history, and geography. The school bell rings at 10:00 A.M., signaling the end of class. By that time, it's hot outside, making it tough to concentrate on schoolwork in the warm classrooms. Students go home for lunch and an afternoon rest. At 3:00 kids go back to class until 5:00.

At age 12, some children get jobs or help out on the family farm. Others go on to secondary school for seven years. A major exam marks the end of secondary school. If students pass this very tough exam, they receive a high school diploma.

Students in a Malagasy classroom take a test while a teacher looks on. Hope they studied!

School's out! Students fill the playground on their way home for the day.

Fady

Outside of school, there are cultural rules that kids and adults must follow. In Madagascar things that people should not do are called *fady*. People in different areas of Madagascar follow different sets of fady. Here are a few examples.

Being rude to a stranger is fady.

For a stranger to refuse kindness and hospitality is fady.

At meals, children eating before their elders do is fady.

Eating certain foods could be fady.

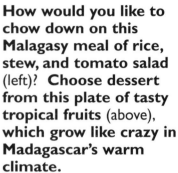

How would you like to chow down on this Malagasy meal of rice, stew, and tomato salad (left)? **Choose dessert from this plate of tasty tropical fruits** (above), which grow like crazy in Madagascar's warm climate.

Let's Eat **Rice**

Most Malagasy eat their meals while seated on straw mats on the floor. And you won't find a fork or a knife around—a spoon is all you'll need. What's on the menu? Rice—it thrives in rice paddies all over the island, and it's the most popular food in Madagascar. Folks usually eat rice for breakfast, lunch, and dinner. Diners fill up on watery rice for breakfast. For lunch firmly cooked rice is served with onions or another vegetable. And at dinnertime, heaping mounds of steamed or fried rice are topped with lots of vegetables or with stews chock-full of chicken, fish, or pork. The strong flavors of chili peppers, curry powder, cloves, and garlic spice up the stews. The side dish *lasary voatabia*—tomatoes and onions tossed in a lemon and hot pepper sauce—makes Malagasy mouths water.

Thirsty? Reach for a glass of *rano vola*. This rice water is the drink of choice in Madagascar. To make rano vola, cooks boil water in pots containing the clumps of rice that stick to the bottom and sides of the pan. When cooled and strained, rano vola is ready to drink.

Lasary Voatabia

This side salad is a Malagasy favorite, and it's easy to make. Just be sure to have an adult help with the chopping.

You will need:

2 large tomatoes
2 scallions
1 tablespoon water
1 tablespoon lemon juice

$1/2$ teaspoon salt
pepper to taste
1 drop hot sauce (optional)

Wash the vegetables in cold water. Carefully chop the tomatoes and the scallions into bite-sized pieces. Place the chopped vegetables in a large bowl. Add the water, lemon juice, salt, pepper, and hot sauce. Use a spoon to mix the ingredients. Place in the refrigerator and chill for 1 hour before serving. Makes 6 small salads.

Tell a **Tale**

Listening to stories is a favorite way to pass the time in Madagascar. Books are expensive, and not many are published in the Malagasy language. So the storytelling tradition is popular. Many of the **folktales**—stories that are passed down from grandparents to parents to children—give reasons why things happen in nature or tell how the world began.

Kabary, a kind of Malagasy entertainment, mixes storytelling with speechmaking. Clever speakers talk around the subject and never get straight to the point, making the audience crack up with laughter. Kabary artists use **proverbs** called *ohabolana*. Malagasy speakers might use many of these short, witty sayings in everyday conversation. The Malagasy take pride in being able to find the perfect proverb for every situation. One example of an ohabolana is "Do not kick away the canoe that helped you cross the river," which means "Don't forget the people who helped you get where you are." Another is "Do not waste your time looking for soft ground to dig your shovel into," which means "Don't look for the easy way out."

A Malagasy Folktale

One day long ago, Zanahary asked the first man and woman if they would prefer to die like the moon or like a banana tree. The couple looked at each other in confusion until the woman asked, "What does it mean to die like the moon?"

Zanahary replied, "The moon is always reborn. Each month the moon starts out as a sliver and grows bigger. Then it gets smaller until one night it disappears. The next night it's a sliver again."

The couple thought about this for a moment. Then the man asked, "How does one die like a banana tree?"

"A banana tree sends off shoots. After the tree dies, the shoots continue to live, eventually growing into young trees," answered Zanahary.

So if the couple didn't have children, they could live forever like the moon does. If they did have kids, they would give life to others like the banana tree does. The first couple thought about this choice, and they decided to die like a banana tree. Because of their decision, humans have only one lifetime on earth.

An artist weaves a basket out of palm fronds.

Art All **Over**

In Madagascar you can find art made from wood, grasses, stone, metal, cattle horns, clay, cloth, and even feathers. The artworks reflect the different cultures that make up the Malagasy people. French colonists introduced embroidery and sewing. Malagasy embroiderers make table-cloths and collars for shirts and dresses. Long-ago African settlers

It takes a steady hand to chisel the finishing touches into a wood carving.

40

Zoma Market

A great place to see many of the beautiful handmade Malagasy crafts is at the Zoma Market in Antananarivo. Zoma Market, located in the center of town, is the largest open-air market in the world!

Zoma Market is a busy place where you can find anything—from fruits and vegetables to furniture and flowers. Woven rugs, hats, clothes, wood carvings, musical instruments, toys, and even magic charms are all available for sale.

brought the craft of weaving to the island. People form grass and straw into mats, baskets, and hats. Skilled workers weave cotton into cloth, which is dyed beautiful colors and used for clothing.

Wood carving, another African tradition, has become an important part of Madagascar's culture. The Betsileo people carve furniture from trees found on the island, such as ebony, rosewood, and sandalwood. The most celebrated and unique wood carvings are the tomb posts, called *aloalos*. The Mahafaly people in southern Madagascar carve tall posts with symbols or pictures that represent a dead person's life. The aloalos are colorfully painted and placed on stone tombs.

41

Malagasy musicians strum and sing for an audience.

Belt Out a
Tune

Singing is a big part of traditional Malagasy music. Many of the traditional songs and dances of the Malagasy tell a story. Folks like to sing in harmony. Musicians play along on traditional instruments such as the *valiha* (a type of guitar made from bamboo or wood), the xylophone, and cone-shaped drums. Conch horns, made from big seashells, and flutes sometimes chime in, too.

Traveling musicians go from village to village performing *hira gasy*, a show that mixes storytelling, singing, and dance. The kabary begins the show. The next act is a play in which actors sing their lines. Dancers end the show by performing to the music of trumpets, drums, and violins.

Malagasy music has hints of styles from other countries. On the western side of the island, people tune in to radio stations broadcasting from East Africa. Western Malagasy musicians reflect this influence, punctuating their songs with strong drumbeats. In the Central Highlands, on the other hand, some of the music of the Merina people features stringed instruments, as does the music you might hear in Asian countries.

Salegy

The most popular dance in Madagascar is the *salegy*. The dancers form a line by placing their arms on the shoulders of the dancer next to them. The line moves back and forth together as the music gets faster and faster!

Girls clap, dance, and sing for fun at recess. Care to join in?

Glossary

ancestor: A long-ago relative, such as a great-great-great-grandparent.

canal: A waterway, either natural or artificial, that is used for navigation or irrigation.

cyclone: A severe storm that carries high winds and heavy rains.

ethnic group: A large community of people that shares a number of social features in common, such as language, religion, or customs.

extinct: No longer living.

folktale: A story told within a given culture that explains important ideas—such as where an ethnic group came from or how the world began.

lamba: A long scarf that drapes across the body and ties at the shoulder.

loincloth: A cloth worn around the hips that hangs halfway to the knees.

When Madagascar gained its independence from France in 1960, the new government adopted this flag. White represents pure ideals. Red stands for independence. Green is symbolic of coastal dwellers.

Disappearing Trees

Rain forests once covered most of Madagascar. But many trees have been cut down to make room for farming, for grazing cattle, and for an increasing population. Destroying the forest means that many of Madagascar's unique animals and plants have nowhere to live. Also, without trees, heavy rains wash away much of the soil, making it hard for farmers to grow crops. The government has tried to stop rain forest destruction by setting up national parks to protect some forested areas.

loom: A machine for weaving thread or yarn into cloth.

monsoon: A period of heavy rain brought by seasonal winds.

plain: A broad, flat area of land, usually covered with grass, that has few trees or other outstanding natural features.

proverb: A short, witty saying that offers advice or wisdom.

rain forest: A dense, green forest that receives large amounts of rain every year. These forests lie near the equator.

sacrifice: To kill an animal as an offering to gods or ancestors.

Pronunciation Guide

aepyornis	ee-pee-OR-nuhs
Alahamady	ah-lah-MARD
aloalos	ah-LOOL
Andriamanitra	ahn-dree-ah-MAHN-tray
Antananarivo	ahn-tah-nah-nah-REEV
Betsimisaraka	BET-sih-MIH-shah-rahk
coelacanth	SEE-luh-kanth
fady	FAH-dee
fakonolona	fook-ahn-oh-LOON
famadihana	fah-mah-DEE-ahn
hira gasy	HEE-rah GASH
kabary	kah-BAHR
lamba mena	LAHM-bah MAIN
lasary voatabia	lah-sah-REE voh-tah-BEE
lemur	LEE-mehr
Malagasy	mahl-GASH
Maromokotro	mah-room-KOOT-roh
Merina	MAIR-n
Miteny Gasy ve ianao	meh-TAIN GASH vay yah-NOW
pousse pousse	POOS POOS
rano vola	RAHN-oh VOOL
razana	RAH-zah-nah
taxi-brousse	TAHK-see BROOS
Tongasoa eto Madagasikara	TOON-gah-soo-ah AH-too mah-dah-gahs-KAH-rah
Tsia Fakantitra	SEE-yah fah-KAHN-tee-trah
valiha	vah-LEE-bih
Zanahary	zah-nah-HAR
Zoma	ZOO-mah

Further Reading

Heale, Jay. *Cultures of the World: Madagascar*. New York: Marshall Cavendish, 1998.

Johnson, Sylvia A. *Rice*. Minneapolis: Lerner Publications Company, 1985.

Madagascar in Pictures. Minneapolis: Lerner Publications Company, 1989.

Oldfield, Sara. *Endangered People & Places: Rain Forests*. Minneapolis: Lerner Publications Company, 1996.

Rappaport, Doreen. *The New King*. New York: Dial Books for Young Readers, 1995.

Stevens, Rita. *Places and Peoples of the World: Madagascar*. Philadelphia: Chelsea House Publishers, 1999.

Temko, Florence. *Traditional Crafts from Africa*. Minneapolis: Lerner Publications Company, 1996.

Metric Conversion Chart

WHEN YOU KNOW:	MULTIPLY BY:	TO FIND:
teaspoon	5.0	milliliters
Tablespoon	15.0	milliliters
cup	0.24	liters
inches	2.54	centimeters
feet	0.3048	meters
miles	1.609	kilometers
square miles	2.59	square kilometers
degrees Fahrenheit	5/9 (after subtracting 32)	degrees Celsius

Index